D0812432

WEAPONS OF THE WEST

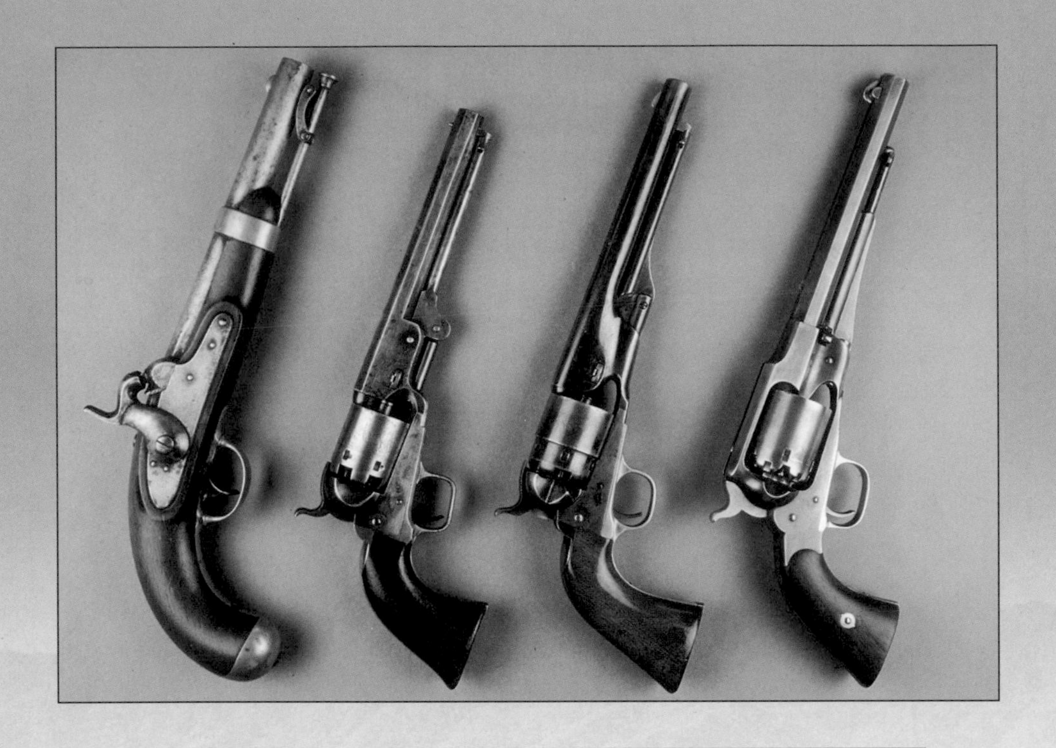

A gunslinger's weapon in the Wild West was often customized and unique. Pictured above from left to right are a Remington revolver with walnut grip, a single-action Colt .44 caliber pistol, a six-shot Colt revolver, and a single-shot percussion pistol.

WEAPONS OF THE WEST

RUSTY FISCHER

Mason Crest Publishers
370 Reed Road
Broomall PA 19008
www.masoncrest.com

 Printed and bound in the
Hashemite Kingdom of Jordan.

First printing

1 3 5 7 9 8 6 4 2

Library of Congress Cataloging-in-Publication Data
on file at the Library of Congress

ISBN 1-59084-066-6

Publisher's note: many of the quotations in this book come from original sources, and contain the spelling and grammatical inconsistencies of the original text.

CONTENTS

Sun filters across a storefront porch in Tombstone, Arizona. This legendary town outlasted some of the most infamous characters of the West, and was the site of the famous gunfight at the O. K. Corral.

GUNFIGHT AT THE O.K. CORRAL

IT WAS A COLD AND OVERCAST DAY ON OCTOBER 26, 1881, WHEN THREE BROTHERS AND a family friend stood nearly toe to toe with some of the meanest gunfighters in the West. It was just one more armed skirmish in a part of the still-young country that was known for gunplay, lawlessness, and violence. The result would eventually come to be known as the gunfight at the O. K. Corral.

But did you know that the entire gunfight lasted less than 60 seconds?

The Earp brothers, Wyatt, Virgil and Morgan, were tough-talking, hard-fighting men who earned their living as lawmen in the lawless territory of the frontier west. Business was good for the Earps, as boomtown after boomtown sprang up on the western frontier as a result of the Homestead Act—a law that allowed Americans to buy land cheaply in the West—as well as the discovery of precious metals such as gold and silver.

The Wild West was full of colorful nicknames for various characters, and "Doc" Holliday is a perfect example. And like the other gunfighters of his era, Holliday's nickname was well earned. In fact, his nickname may have been more meaningful than most—Holliday was called "Doc" because he was a real dentist!

These rowdy towns full of hard-drinking, hard-living men needed someone to keep them under control, and that's just what the Earp brothers were good at. One such boomtown was Tombstone, Arizona, about 50 miles southeast of Tucson. The cramped and dusty city was founded in 1879 as a result of the discovery of silver in the nearby San Pedro Hills.

After the discovery, miners and con men alike flocked to the new city to ply their trades. After only two years, the town boasted nearly 5,500 residents!

Wyatt Earp had served as the assistant city marshal of Dodge City, Kansas. He and his brothers had migrated to Tombstone by 1880. Once they were settled, Virgil became the lawman while his brothers took jobs in local saloons or guarding Wells, Fargo stagecoaches. A family friend, Doc Holliday, joined the Earps in Tombstone and split his time between his career of dentistry and his love of gambling.

However, all was not well in the bustling mining town. While the Earps and Holliday worked at honest, professional trades, another group of tough men lived just outside the law.

One of the most famous lawmen of the West was Wyatt Earp. He was born March 19, 1848, in Monmouth, Illinois; during his childhood, the Earp family moved west several times. They eventually settled in California.

In 1870, Wyatt took his first job as a lawman in the town of Lamar, Missouri. He would go on to become a respected lawman in several Kansas towns, including Wichita and Ellsworth. There was always a lot of action, because the towns were at the end of the cattle trails, so cowboys who had spent grueling weeks driving cattle tended to come into town and get a bit rowdy. But Wyatt gained a reputation as a man who did not have to use his gun to resolve problems and enforce the laws. In 1876, he became an assistant city marshal in Dodge City, Kansas.

By 1879, Wyatt Earp had tamed Dodge City, so he left looking for a new challenge. He joined his older brother, Virgil, in the grimly named town of Tombstone, Arizona. Virgil was Tombstone's marshal, and he appointed Wyatt a deputy. On October 26, 1881, Wyatt, Virgil, and Morgan Earp, as well as their friend Doc Holliday, participated in the gunfight at the O. K. Corral against the Clantons and McLaurys.

Two months after the gun battle, friends of the McLaurys ambushed Virgil Earp. Though Virgil was not killed, he was crippled for life. In March 1882, McLaury supporters killed Morgan Earp. Wyatt promised he would get even. With a group of friends he found and killed the men who had attacked his brothers.

Now on the wrong side of the law, Wyatt left Tombstone. He spent the next few years drifting from place to place. He opened a saloon in Alaska, and hunted for gold in Nevada. He eventually became a bounty hunter working with the Los Angeles police department. Wyatt Earp died on January 13, 1929.

Wyatt Earp (left) and Doc Holliday were close friends. They had met when Wyatt was working as a lawman in Dodge City. Doc Holliday was suffering from tuberculosis, a disease of the lungs. He moved to Arizona hoping the dry climate would improve his health.

Ike and Billy Clanton and Tom and Frank McLaury were two sets of brothers who liked to have a good time, whether what they were doing was legal or not!

Almost from the beginning, the two sides clashed. Wyatt Earp's horse was stolen and, eventually, Billy Clanton was caught riding it. Then, mules that had been stolen from a nearby army post wound up at the McLaurys' ranch. When the Earps became part of a federal **posse** that eventually helped locate the missing mules, the McLaury brothers swore that they'd get even with the Earps.

On the morning of the shoot-out, Virgil had arrested Ike Clanton for possessing firearms within the city limits, a law that was often broken and rarely enforced. While taking Ike

Three men were killed during the gunfight at the O. K. Corral. Frank McLaury (left) was shot by both Wyatt and Morgan Earp. Tom McLaury (center) was killed by a shotgun blast from Doc Holliday. Billy Clanton (right) had tried to talk Ike Clanton (bottom) out of confronting the Earps. Billy was killed by two bullets fired by Morgan Earp, while Ike escaped the fray without injury.

to court, Virgil hit him over the head with his **revolver**. After Ike paid a fine and was released, he ran into Billy Clanton and Frank McLaury. Billy wanted Ike to go home, but Ike, in a foul mood from Virgil's head cracking, resisted. Tom McLaury joined the group, which stood, fully armed, on the city's main street.

The Earps and Doc Holliday gathered across the street, about three houses away from the Clanton and McLaury gang, and decided to arrest the whole lot of them for carrying weapons. The local sheriff, sensing trouble, tried to talk the Earps out of confronting the armed men. However, the brothers, along with Doc Holliday, brushed him aside and headed straight for the **cowboys**.

Actually, the gunfight itself did not take place at or even near the famed O. K. Corral. In fact, it took place about half a block from the corral, in a scruffy yard less than 30 feet wide between a private home and a photo gallery.

As was the case with most gunfights of the West, the weapons for both sides were shotguns and pistols. It is unclear exactly which gunfighter used which weapon, but most witnesses attested to the fact that both sides were fully armed. By all accounts, the gunfight took place at about noon, a possible source for the term "high noon."

When the Earps and Holliday confronted the Clanton and McLaury brothers, the **outlaws** quickly found that they had accidentally boxed themselves in. Stuck between the house

and the photo gallery, there was no place to evade the lawmen. The outlaws were trapped!

Guns were drawn and fired. When the smoke cleared, Tom and Frank McLaury and Billy Clanton lay dead. Ike Clanton escaped. Holliday had been shot in the hip, Morgan Earp was wounded in the shoulder and Virgil Earp had been hit in the leg. Only Wyatt remained untouched, a fact that added to his reputation as one of the fiercest gunfighters in the West.

Few who were present that day realized that the gunfight near the O. K. Corral would go down in history as one of the defining moments of the West. But over the years, eyewitness accounts, books, and even Hollywood movies have contributed to the legend that has become the Gunfight at the O. K. Corral.

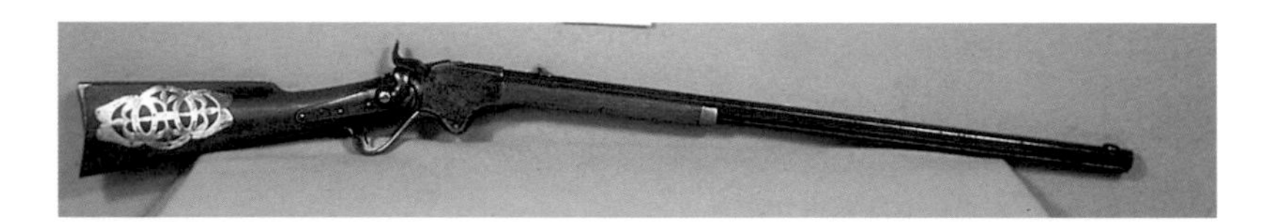

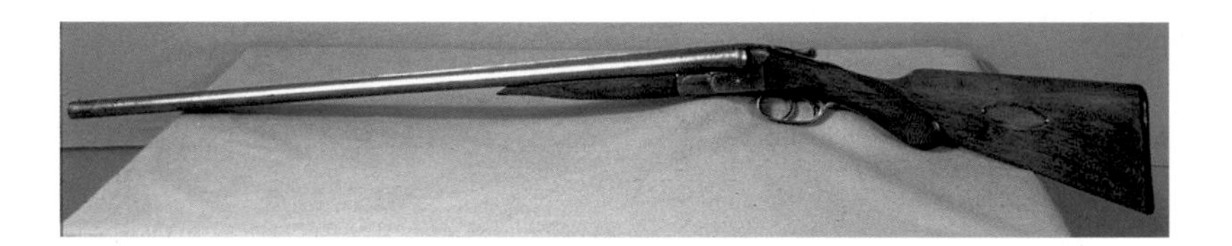

Three of the guns that helped to tame the West. The Colt Navy .36 revolver (top) was a common sidearm for officers during the Civil War; many veterans took their guns with them as they moved west after the war. The 1864 .44 Spencer carbine (center) was a popular repeating rifle, and was the forerunner of the Winchester rifle developed in 1873. A shotgun, such as this double-barreled Spencer Arms model from the late 1880s (bottom), provided a lot of firepower at close range. Within a range of about 40 yards, a shotgun blast could practically cut a man in half.

2 GUNS BLAZING

JESSE JAMES. DOC HOLLIDAY. BILLY THE KID. WYATT EARP. THESE FAMOUS MEN AND HISTORICAL figures were just a few of the gunfighters whose names would evoke images of fast hands, cold eyes, and lethal weapons still smoking in their hands while a victim lay dying in the dirt. These men were masters of their trade—marksmen with an ability to hit whatever they were aiming at, again and again, with lightning speed.

Gunfighters became the new royalty in the Wild West, and while many of the tales surrounding them may have become exaggerated with time and the telling, few can dispute the fact that the West was a dangerous place to be when two rival gunslingers wanted to settle a score!

But gunfighting was a new phenomenon in America, thanks to the development of handguns, most notably the revolver.

The guns of the West came in as many varieties as the men who wore them, but the most common tool of the traditional gunfight was a **single-action** revolver with a barrel that was shorter than five inches. These guns were lighter and easier to handle than most other guns of this time period, and their small size allowed them to be worn at all times and drawn quickly if trouble should arise.

Samuel Colt was an inventor and manufacturer from Connecticut who patented the first revolver-type handgun at his plant in Patterson, New Jersey. His .36 caliber revolver, patented in 1836, was a great success. Colt wasn't finished perfecting the handgun, however. He took suggestions on how to improve the gun from Captain Samuel H. Walker of the Texas Rangers. Those improvements were incorporated into a new model, first issued in 1847. The Walker Colt was a more powerful weapon.

After receiving a government contract for more than 1,000 of the revolvers for use in the Mexican War (1846–1848), Colt opened another weapons plant in Connecticut. Sales of Colt's guns soared during the Civil War.

In 1873, the Colt Patent Fine Arms Company moved away from percussion cap-fired ammunition (loose powder and ball in a paper cartridge) to the newly invented metal cartridge containing its own primer, powder, and bullet at the end of a copper or brass tube. The first pistol to fire this new ammo was the Colt Peacemaker, which is often referred to as "the gun that won the West."

A gun's "action" refers to the machinery that actually fires the cartridges, or bullets. It also controls the way the bullets are loaded into the firing chamber and how the empty cases are removed. Until the 1830s, most weapons were muzzle-loading **muskets**. Once they were fired, the soldier or gunman had to stop what he was doing to reload. That was a long process. First the soldier would pour **gunpowder** into the barrel, followed by a piece of cloth called wadding. Then a bullet or musket ball would be loaded down the barrel of the gun. Then the soldier could take their firearm back up, aim it, and fire. Lots of things could happen in such a long amount of time and not many of them were good.

Gunfighters were called by many different names. These names included "shootists," "leather slappers," "gun fanners," and "gun tippers." But one word described them all: dangerous!

In a **flintlock** pistol, a small piece of flint was attached to a hammer, which had a thumb cocking mechanism. A small portion of powder was placed in a flash pan, while a lock was pulled down over this powder to protect it. When the trigger was pulled, it released the hammer so that the flint struck the lock, flipping it out of the way of the pan while at the same time creating a sizable spark. This spark ignited the gunpowder and, finally, launched the bullet. While not as slow as muzzle-loading guns, there was still much room for improvement.

That improvement was thanks largely to one man: Samuel Colt.

As someone once said in the West, "Abe Lincoln may have freed all men, but Sam Colt made them equal." This post-Civil War slogan referred to the very unique gun that forever linked Sam Colt's name to revolvers. In 1836, Sam Colt received a U.S. patent for the Colt firearm. The idea for this revolutionary gun

Contrary to popular opinion, not all revolvers were "short" guns. Rifles, which are definitely long guns, have been built using a revolving cylinder to hold the bullets before they are fired. However, the word *revolver* is generally used to describe a shorter handgun that uses a cylindrical magazine called the "cylinder" to hold up to six bullets. Since the cylinder "revolves" as each bullet is shot, it is this cylinder that gives the revolver its name.

is said to have come to Colt when he was serving as a seaman aboard the sailing ship *Corvo*.The Colt pistol was equipped with a revolving **cylinder** that could hold up to six bullets.

The cylinder is at the rear end of the gun's barrel, with several holes (usually six) bored through it, pointing in the same direction as the gun's barrel. Each time the cylinder rotates, one of these holes is always behind the barrel. This, in effect, forms an extension of the barrel when the cylinder is in place. When the gun is loaded, a bullet is placed in each hole.

When the single bullet in the hole behind the barrel is fired, the cylinder automatically rotates so that the next bullet lines up with the barrel and is ready to be fired immediately. The bullet is fired when the trigger, located under the cylinder, is pulled, releasing a hammer behind the frame, which uses spring pressure to cause it to move forward and hit the firing pin. This pin, in turn, strikes the primer on the bullet. This primer, much like the head of a match, explodes, setting off the gunpowder found inside the casing of the bullet.

Colt's revolver provided its user with greatly increased firepower. Prior to his invention, only one- and two-barrel flintlock pistols were available. Some 19th-century historians have gone so far as to say that Sam Colt's invention altered the course of history. To this day, the name Colt still suggests firearms to most Americans.

As Colt's invention gave gunfighters expanded firepower and more reliable guns, it also gave them choices. For instance, would they choose a single-action or a **double-action** revolver? The difference between double- and single-action revolvers is that double-action revolvers cock and release the hammer with a single pull of the trigger, whereas

One of the most popular guns ever sold in the West was the 1873 Colt .45 Peacemaker. The weapon was popular with both lawmen and outlaws; this nickle-plated, ivory-handled Peacemaker belonged to Wyatt Earp.

single-action revolvers have to be cocked by pulling the hammer back. In both cases, when the gun is uncocked the hammer will be in contact with the chamber underneath it. If that chamber is loaded, a sudden, sharp blow to the hammer will cause the round to fire. This is why very few gunmen loaded all six cylinders in their revolvers!

With a single-action revolver, the cylinder is moved into position to fire the next bullet by the shooter pulling back, or cocking, the hammer of the gun. With a double-action revolver, the cylinder can be moved into position by the first part of the trigger pull, which also cocks the hammer at the same time.

This made the double-action revolver quicker on the draw, but less accurate due to the force necessary to pull the trigger, which was actually working twice as hard. The single-action revolver, on the other hand, was slower on the draw, but more accurate. Gunfighters were free to choose which option they preferred, speed or accuracy. Sometimes, by owning two guns, they chose both!

Caliber, or bore size, is the diameter of the inside of the barrel expressed in inches. Thus .44 caliber means 44/100 of an inch.

The gunfighter was a man who lived on the edge. Despite the advances made by Sam Colt and other gun manufacturers toward the end of the 19th century, gun making was still an

The holster was an important piece of equipment to the fighting man in the west. This is an example of a crossdraw holster; the butt of the gun is facing forward, and the gunman would draw his pistol with his opposite hand.

inexact science. Inventors all over the country were dreaming up new guns, ammunition, **holsters**, and other inventions. But shoddy equipment and cheap materials meant that, unless a gun had been tested and tried in a gunfighter's able hands, it couldn't be trusted.

Gunfighters had more to worry about than just faulty revolvers, however. Even the best gunfighters fell prey to outside factors beyond their control, such as dust, wind, or sunshine. Exploding gunpowder and speeding bullets didn't stop because a gunfighter had to sneeze in the middle of a showdown or if the sun got in his eyes! Death was always around the corner for a gunfighter, and these men knew it.

As such, their hangouts were places where they could relax and escape the stresses of their unique profession. Bars and saloons teemed with pistol-packing patrons just trying to let off a little steam. Unfortunately, a room full of gunslingers often led to trouble, and deserted streets weren't the only places where showdowns occurred.

Guns were very plentiful, and easy to get, in the Old West, whether traded for a jug of whiskey, bought at the local dry goods store or mercantile, or even ordered through the mail! This meant that anyone could own one, not to mention wear one, and too much whiskey and a new gun served to make bad gunfighters out of many good men.

Competitors of the Colt Patent Fire Arms Company included Remington, Smith & Wesson, Springfield Arms, and the Winchester Repeating Arms Company.

Professional gunfighters, however, usually came from fields where guns were a big part of the job: law officers, cowboys, ranchers, farmers, rustlers, hired guns, soldiers, miners, scouts, bounty hunters, and other dangerous professions.

Almost as important to a gunfighter as his expert vision, fast hands, and, of course, his gun, was the draw. The draw was the act of taking one's gun out of a holster and firing it, all in one smooth motion. This is where the term "fast on the draw" comes from. The faster a gunfighter could draw his gun, the sooner he could get his revolver up, aimed, and fired.

In 1870 a French company manufactured a "turret" revolver. This gun used a round wheel, or turret, to hold 10 bullets. It was a large, cumbersome weapon that never quite caught on in America.

While it may seem simple, drawing one's gun consisted of much more than simply pulling the gun out of its holster. Each gunfighter had a unique way of drawing that suited his particular style. Some gunfighters relied on speed, drawing quickly and aiming poorly. Others drew more slowly—though far from slow—and aimed with deadly accuracy.

One unique type of draw was called "**border style**." This draw consisted of pulling your pistol, worn backward in the holster, by reaching your arm across the front of your body. This draw got its name because it was most popular around the Mexican border.

Of course, gunfighters would have been lost without another tool of their trade, the holsters that held their precious guns. These leather "carrying cases" for guns were durable and convenient. They allowed the gunfighter instant access to his gun at anytime, day or night. The most common type of holster was the standard, open-top holster that hung straight down the gunfighter's leg when suspended from his gun belt. However, there were as many different types of holsters as there were gunfighters.

The **crossdraw** holster was just like the standard holster except for the fact that the butt of the gun faced forward. While it may have looked odd to the uninformed, real gunfighters knew that this holster was a sure sign that its owner spent a lot of time in the saddle. After all, despite how easy it looks in the movies, it was not very easy to draw from a standard holster while riding a horse across sagebrush and dirt. The crossdraw holster solved this problem by allowing the cowboy or lawman to draw more quickly by reaching across his body instead of straight down at his side.

Samuel Colt died in 1863, ten years before his company came up with its most popular revolver, the 1873 Colt Peacemaker. The Colt company would produce 357,859 Peacemakers.

Probably the most popular holsters with gunfighters were "fast-draw" holsters. As their name implies, fast-draw holsters resembled standard holsters, except for the fact that they tilted the gun barrel forward slightly. This allowed a gunfighter to avoid shooting himself in the foot if he was a little too quick on the draw. It is a little-known fact that sweat, sand, dust, and nervousness often contributed to a gunfighter, even an experienced one, shooting himself before he ever shot someone else!

Gunfighters weren't the types to turn away from any holster that might give them even the slightest advantage over their opponent. For example, something known as a "swivel" holster was attached to the gun belt by way of a swivel. Even better, the bottom of the holster remained open so that the gunfighter could shoot through it! All he had to do to make the gun ready for firing was to push back and down on the butt and slide his finger on the trigger. A good gunfighter with this kind of holster was as fast as lightning, and very hard to outdraw.

Remington's Frontier model .44 was considered by many to be second only to the Colt Peacemaker for quality. Some liked the Frontier best. "The Remington is the hardest and the surest shooting pistol made," Jesse James claimed.

3 COWBOY JUSTICE

ONE OF THE BIGGEST CHARACTERS TO COME OUT OF THE OLD WEST WAS THE COWBOY. LARGER than life, the cowboy spent his days herding cattle, tending to his horse, and trying to get enough food to keep him full of energy on his long, 14-hour days. This rugged hero was a take-charge fellow who handled his problems in his own, unique way. He could watch a herd of 1,000 cattle and know which ones were getting fidgety and likely to stray. He could handle a horse like a racecar, stopping on a dime or racing across the dusty trails to turn the herd. But a cowboy's life wasn't all prairie songs and romance. Danger often lurked, and the cowboy had to be ready for it.

Each day, a cowboy faced the risk of broken bones, crippling accidents, and even death. Very few ranches were near a town with a doctor, and so a cowboy had to fend for

Many cowboys found the saddle holster more convenient than a conventional holster. With it, the cowboy's weapon was placed where the cowboy could easily draw it while riding.

After the Civil War, ranchers in the west realized they could make great profits—if they could get their cattle east. One of the primary responsibilities of cowboys was to drive the cattle from Texas and other southwestern states to such Kansas towns as Dodge, Wichita, and Abilene. From there the cattle could be shipped to slaughterhouses in Chicago and the east.

himself in times of sickness or worse. Wild or untamed horses often threw their riders, and a bad fall could easily break a cowboy's leg. With no one around, a cowboy often had to "heal" himself with a makeshift splint of broken twigs tied with his bandana! Unfortunately, a broken bone that was improperly set could leave a cowboy crippled for life.

Roping cattle could mean the loss of a finger if the cowboy's hand got caught between the rope and the horn of his trusty saddle, while a strong, powerful kick from a horse could kill a cowboy in an instant.

The first cowboys were not from America at all: they came from Mexico. These native Mexicans were hard, rugged men who rode on horses and took care of huge herds of cattle. In their own country, they were known as *vaqueros*, which is the Spanish word for "cowboys." When the *vaqueros* began to move their cattle north into America to graze, American ranch hands watched the *vaqueros* and slowly began to copy them.

American cowboys got their start in the border state of Texas. There, cattle grew wild and had few natural enemies. In fact, by the end of the Civil War there were an estimated 5 million of head of cattle in Texas.

Almost a quarter of all cowboys in the United States were African American, and another quarter were Mexican. Many of the black cowboys moved to the Western frontier to escape prejudice and racism after the Civil War, which had recently ended. Others had been slaves on Texas ranches before they were granted their freedom. Many of the Mexican cowboys had remained in Texas after it became a state in 1845. As a result of this unique blend of African American, Mexican, and white men, a sense of equality slowly developed among cowboys because of the hard work and danger they shared equally.

As western ranchers discovered cattle could survive the cold winters in the northern Great Plains, ranches eventually sprang up in Montana, Wyoming, Colorado, and the Dakotas,

Only in the movies did a gunfighter draw his gun and fire off all six shots by snapping back the hammer with his hands! In real life, sweaty palms and unreliable weapons made this practice a truly deadly one.

which had almost no settlers at that time. Long, backbreaking trail drives were used to stock northern ranches with valuable cattle. Naturally, cowboys moved north with the cattle.

There were great profits to be made if the ranchers could get their cattle to markets in the East. A steer worth four dollars in Texas was worth nearly 10 times that much when it was shipped east. Beginning in 1866, the ranchers began moving long lines of cattle northward.

Indians and farmers who resented these cattle drives were upset. Vicious outlaws stole some of the cattle and were not against gunning down the men who were driving them. For this reason, cowboys first became known as gun-toting desperadoes who were quick to aim and even faster to shoot. However, this reputation was not entirely deserved.

A cattle drive was a tremendous undertaking, with thousands of huge beasts tramping across fertile ground, raising dust and tempers as property lines were crossed without regard to feelings or growing crops. Native Americans, already weary of being moved farther off of their native homes by the white man, grew even more resentful as these new trespassers began inching across their new homes.

Of course, trouble brewed as farmers and Indians squared off against the cowboys and their hungry, trampling herds of cattle. While reports of violence between the "cowboys and Indians" of legend have been greatly exaggerated, the threat of danger was always there. For this reason, a cowboy and his gun were rarely parted on a cattle drive.

A cowboy's gun was a big part of his image. With his fancy hat and leather chaps, jingling spurs and rugged, outdoorsy appearance, a cowboy always cut a striking figure when he came into town to buy much-needed supplies. For show, most cowboys carried a revolver with six chambers, known as a **six-shooter**. Much like the gunfighters, the cowboys

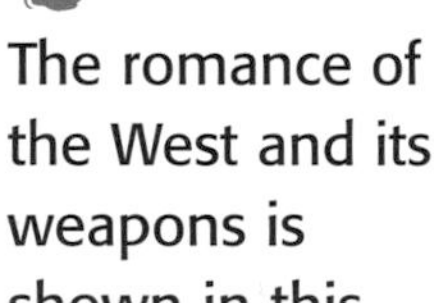

The romance of the West and its weapons is shown in this Smith & Wesson poster from the late 19th century.

One of the most famous cowboys was an African American named **Nat Love**, better known by the nickname Deadwood Dick. Love was born a slave in Davidson County, Tennessee, in 1854. After the Civil War, when he was 15 years old, he left home and went to work as a cowboy near Dodge City, Kansas. He received his nickname after he won a riding, roping, and shooting contest in the town of Deadwood, South Dakota in 1876. Love worked on cattle drives until 1889, and he became a railroad porter in 1890. His autobiography, *The Life and Adventures of Nat Love, Better Known in the Cattle Country as Deadwood Dick*, contains many cowboy stories. It also includes tales about such famous Western characters as Bat Masterson, Billy the Kid, Buffalo Bill, and Jesse James. Like many other legends of the Old West, Love's true adventures are difficult to distinguish from the "tall tales" he told in his book.

appreciated the revolver's small size and effective firepower. A trusty gunbelt and plenty of bullets completed the cowboy's impressive appearance and made him an instant presence in most cow towns, which were otherwise populated by storekeepers and bartenders. Once their business was attended to, many cowboys whiled away the sociable hours in a dusty saloon.

Contrary to popular legend, however, a cowboy did not always carry his gun during his everyday work. After all, a gun could be a big nuisance to a man on horseback. It added extra weight and got in the way, especially as he was roping and branding cattle. Between their chaps and spurs, hats and bandanas, boots and buckles, cowboys had enough accessories to keep them busy! Trail drives, however, were another matter.

On a trail drive, as a cowboy herded 1,000 or more cattle through the desolate stretches of unsettled territory, a cowboy's gun was as valuable as his horse. The farmers and Indians who resented his presence on their land provided the constant fear of danger, and the cowboy always had to be prepared. For this reason, a cowboy often carried two guns on a trail drive. His revolver was handy in his freshly oiled gun belt. After all, an easy-to-reach revolver was useful for killing rattlesnakes, shooting a horse with a broken leg, and even turning back stampeding cattle.

There was a second gun, however, that most cowboys kept tucked into their bedrolls, just in case. The bedroll, which usually consisted of a rugged blanket and a few cooking utensils, was usually rolled up and attached directly behind the saddle. As a result, this second gun became known as his "saddle gun."

One such **rifle** was the popular Spencer rifle. This revolutionary repeating rifle had become famous for its use during the Civil War, and was followed up by the Spencer company with the popular Spencer carbine. That is, until Oliver Winchester bought out the Spencer Company and then produced the famous Winchester '73 rifle in 1873. Considered by many to be the most famous rifle of all time, it was developed by the famous John Moses Browning of Utah.

In the longer barrel of the Winchester '73 rifle, the cartridge gained more power than it did along the shorter barrel of the six-gun. This was helpful to cowboys on the open plain, who could see trouble coming from a mile away. Also, the Winchester rifle was easier to aim, and held more cartridges than the six-gun.

The Winchester rifle could also be carried with its hammer down on a round in the chamber, making it safer than a fully-loaded revolver. A center-fire repeating rifle, the Winchester could be fired rapidly and at long ranges, a fact which made quite a few Winchester rifle-owning cowboys feel safer on the cattle trail. Therefore, the gun known as the Winchester rifle was hands-down the cowboy's favorite companion on the hot and dusty trail—besides his trusty horse, that is!

Guns were not the only weapons a world-weary cowboy carried along the long, dusty cattle trail, however. After all, it was the rare cowboy who didn't travel with a knife tucked away somewhere convenient, such as in his saddle roll, stuck in his gun belt, or even hidden in his saddle. Knives were handy tools on the trail. They were used for cutting rope, plugs of chewing tobacco, or pesky spurs from a horse's hide or mane, but they could also be used in combat when a cowboy's bullets ran out. Despite the notion of cowboys and Indians racing at each other with guns drawn, a cattle trail was a long, arduous journey and, though he was careful to have at least one gun handy, a cowboy couldn't stock many rounds of ammunition, even in his saddle roll or bags. A loaded revolver and the bullets on his gun belt would have to suffice, and once they were gone, there weren't any general stores on the trail to offer him new ones. A knife was always loaded, and few cowboys were afraid to use them.

Cowboys spent most of their working hours in the saddle. Horses not only enabled cowboys to cover great distances but also helped them control the cattle. Such horses, however, were large, powerful beasts that had to be tamed before they could be ridden, especially along the great expanse of a cattle trail. However, cowboys were expert horse handlers and, when necessary, could use their horses as secret weapons, sticking their spurs into their haunches and forcing them to rise up against a standing enemy with hooves kicking. Cowboys even used their horses as shields, as a last resort, when ambushed on the open trail with little other cover available.

A homesteader guards his belongings with a rifle slung over his shoulder. Guns were used to deter others as often as they were actually utilized as weapons.

4 KEEPING THE PEACE

THE WEST WASN'T MADE UP ENTIRELY OF GUNFIGHTERS AND COWBOYS. MANY OF the people who lived there were hardworking, honest farmers and settlers. As boomtowns popped up all over the West and the Homestead Act made it possible for farmers to own their own land, entire wagon trains full of hopeful dreamers headed out west through such famous passages as the Oregon Trail.

Once there, however, they often found life harder than they expected. Though the presence of marauding tribes of Indians and cutthroat bandits has been greatly exaggerated, there was a strong sense of loneliness and fear on the new frontier. Homesteads were often miles apart from each other. With no neighbors to hear one's cries for help or to rush to one's aid, a hardworking farm family had to rely on itself for defense. Naturally, it was common for such families to arm themselves, much as the gunfighters and cowboys did, with at least one pistol or revolver for personal protection and one rifle for long-range fire, to aim at such dangers as approaching cattle rustlers or Indians. The rifle could also be used by the homesteaders to put fresh meat on their tables by hunting.

But while farm families might have lived relatively quiet lives, crime was common in the mining camps and cattle towns where lots of people lived close together. These isolated boomtowns sometimes contained great riches in silver and gold and attracted many con men and thieves. Others meant well, but a mixture of gambling, drinking, and firearms often led to trouble.

The Oregon Trail was a 2,000-mile route west followed by thousands of pioneers in the 1840s and 1850s. Starting from towns on the Missouri River like Independence, Westport, and St. Joseph, wagon trains would follow the trail westward to where the Blue River meets the Platte River. The Oregon Trail then followed the south bank of the Platte to the Sweetwater River, which led to South Pass in Wyoming. Continuing along the Bear, Boise, and Snake rivers, travelers eventually reached the Columbia River. This took them to land in the Oregon Territory, which included the present-day states of Washington and Oregon.

It was a long, hard journey; many pioneers kept a loaded rifle under the seat of their wagon, where it could easily be reached if danger appeared. The settlers moving west also had to rely on their shooting skills in order to provide fresh game for their families.

Crime often resulted from the temptations of gold and silver found in these bustling, yet mostly unprotected, boomtowns. Successful miners who had struck it rich usually celebrated by hitting the saloons. Few kept quiet about their newly mined fortunes. Once intoxicated, these miners might be stabbed and robbed. Or a player with a deck full of marked cards could cheat them in a poker game.

Although modern revolvers could hold six bullets in their cylinder, experienced gunfighters only loaded five. The empty cylinder was under the hammer of the gun. This prevented accidents should the hammer inadvertently get pulled back and released!

Gold and silver also tempted armed bandits, who followed stagecoach shipments on their dangerous way west. They picked a deserted spot in which to attack a wagon or stagecoach. Such outlaws usually worked together in gangs, such as the Dalton Gang or the James Gang. These dangerous men robbed banks, trains, and stagecoaches for a living. It is said that Sam Bass once stole $60,000 in gold from a single Union Pacific train.

One target for such bandits is, amazingly, still around today: Wells, Fargo & Company. Henry Wells and William G. Fargo founded the company in 1852. Wells, Fargo & Company carried passengers, freight, and mail. However, it specialized in shipping gold and silver from western mines. Lured by the promise of striking it rich, bands of outlaws

This Wells, Fargo wagon is loaded with $250,000 worth of gold bullion. Five guards armed with loaded shotguns are present to protect the gold from bandits. This practice led to the phrase "riding shotgun."

hovered around the Wells, Fargo trade routes. As a result, the company hired armed guards to protect the precious cargo from these hoodlums on horseback. Up to six guards, each toting powerful rifles such as the Spencer rifle or the Winchester rifle, rode "shotgun" over whatever they might be carrying.

The **Pony Express** was also dangerous. A mail delivery service that operated between Missouri and California in the early 1860s, the Pony Express consisted of relays of men riding fast ponies or horses that carried letters and small packages across a 1,966-mile trail. These riders could deliver mail to California in 10 days or less, faster than any other mail service of that time.

Only young, lightweight men served as Pony Express riders. Many of them, in fact, were still teenagers. A day's work consisted of a trip of 75 miles or more! The rider carried mail in a specially designed leather saddlebag, which fit over the saddle. The Pony Express ran day and night. Riders worked in all kinds of weather and faced the threat of Indian attacks and roving outlaws who thought the young men might be carrying cash from one point to the

☛ Pony Express riders had a dangerous job. To save weight they were not allowed to carry much equipment. The best-armed riders only carried a revolver and a knife. This young rider, Frank Webner, is wearing a holster on his right side.

Movies often show a gunfighter shooting two guns at the same time, but that rarely happened. Most gunfighters, like boxers or baseball players, have one dominant hand. Whether it be the right one or the left one, a gunfighter's concentration could rarely be wasted on trying to fire two guns at the same time!

next. As a result, most of the riders carried a pair of pistols and a knife, just in case.

When frontier settlers arrived in the unorganized territory known as the West, they brought with them federal, state, and local laws from their former homes back east. But these laws were not always appropriate for their new homes. Often the laws did not take into account new and different situations on the rugged frontier, such as cattle rustling, claim jumping, or card cheats.

Even when laws applied to a community, however, enforcing those laws could often be difficult because of the vast distances between one settlement and another. Often, single sheriffs or marshals were responsible for law and order in settlements that were 100 or more miles away from each other! And even if the sheriff did capture a criminal and bring him to justice, there was often no real jail in which to keep the prisoner.

But law-abiding people lived in all parts of the frontier, and sooner or later they established order by hiring lawmen suited for the job. In fact, frontier towns in the West often found law officers as tough and fearless as the outlaws themselves, such as the famous Earps of Tombstone fame and Pat Garrett, the man who shot Billy the Kid.

While guns were readily available in the Wild West, they weren't always cheap. Gunfighters, despite their romantic reputation, weren't exactly rolling in money. While some of the more famous gunmen preferred ivory grips and fancy engravings on their gun barrels, they often held onto these ornate guns for quite a long time.

There were several reasons for this. One was that gunfighters, like gamblers and other folks who live outside the law, were a superstitious bunch. Few were willing to part with their "lucky" guns, most of which had literally saved their lives. Also, gun manufacturing was still a tricky business in the 19th century. Few aimed as precisely as today's models, and it took awhile for a gunfighter to get used to sighting his weapon so that the bullet would go exactly where he wanted it to go. For professional and safety reasons, gunfighters preferred to hold onto the weapons they were most familiar with. They didn't go buying new guns as often as one might imagine.

Cowboys, on the other hand, were a generally poor lot. While it was true that many a cowboy was rolling in dough right after a cattle trail, that same cowpoke was often scraping by for months afterward! As such, cowboys kept their trusty guns a long time as well.

Frontier families used their guns for protection, but had no

Pat Garrett was born in Chambers County, Alabama, in 1850. He grew up in Louisiana and worked as a cowboy and buffalo hunter in Texas before moving to New Mexico. Garrett, a rancher and sheriff in the West, is best known for killing the outlaw Billy the Kid. Garrett was elected sheriff of Lincoln County, New Mexico, in 1880. As sheriff, he captured his one-time friend Billy the Kid, who had been accused of murder. However, Billy escaped from jail just before he was to be executed. In July 1881, Garrett caught up with the Kid in Fort Sumner, a military post in New Mexico, and shot him to death during a cleverly disguised ambush. After killing Billy the Kid, Garrett became a rancher. He later worked as a tax collector, and wrote a book about the Kid. Garrett was shot to death by a New Mexico rancher named Wayne Brazel. Some people suspect that the rancher and his associates murdered Garrett out of revenge for his killing Billy the Kid.

need for anything fancy, and thus rarely needed to invest in a new gun. Lawmen, on the other hand, saw guns as part of their business, and as such required the latest and the greatest to aid them in their endless search for frontier justice. Fortunately, in the latter part of the 19th century, frontier lawmen had a lot to choose from.

Sam Colt, already famous for his revolutionary five- and six-shooter revolvers, struck gold again with the 1873 Colt Peacemaker. This .45-caliber pistol has long been considered "the gun that won the West." Turned out by the Colt Fire Arms Manufacturing Company of Hartford, Connecticut, it sold for $17 by mail order. More than 350,000 of this popular handgun were sold.

But the inventors at the Colt company weren't the only ones making headway in the West. The Model 1873 Winchester rifle, which introduced lever action for ease and convenience in the lawmen's fiery gun battles, also debuted that year.

Another new player on the scene that would go onto become synonymous with expert weaponry was E. Remington & Sons. Over the years, this partnership developed the first hammerless solid-breech repeating shotgun, the first hammerless autoloading shotgun, the first successful high-power slide-action repeating rifle, and the first lock-breach autoloading rifle. In 1866, Remington produced the state-of-the-art Rolling Block Rifle.

One more emerging company, Smith & Wesson, was founded by two men who shared a dream of developing a new type of firearm, one capable of being fired repeatedly without the annoyance of having to reload with loose powder, ball and primer. Although they were not alone in this endeavor, over the years the partnership of Horace Smith and Daniel B. Wesson manufactured a lever-action pistol that had a tubular magazine that fired a fully self-contained cartridge.

Jesse Woodson James was born in Clay County, Missouri, in 1847. He was the son of a Baptist minister, but quickly turned to a life of crime. During the Civil War, he and his older brother, Frank, joined bands of thieves led by Confederate sympathizers. After the war, Jesse and Frank James formed a new band of outlaws with their cousins, the Youngers, and began to hold up trains, stagecoaches, and banks. In 1871, bank officials hired a famous detective agency to capture Jesse and his gang. In 1875, a bomb thrown into his mother's house, where lawmen thought he was hiding, ended up injuring his mother instead. In 1881, Governor Thomas Crittenden of Missouri offered a $5,000 reward for the arrest of Frank or Jesse James. A member of the James' own gang, Robert Ford, believed he could collect the reward if he killed either brother, and shot Jesse in the head. Jesse died the same day, April 3, 1882, in St. Joseph, Missouri.

In this new "repeating" pistol, the level loaded the pistol and cocked the hammer. It could be fired as rapidly as the lever could be pulled. The firepower of this lever-action pistol was so impressive that in 1854, when the gun was reviewed by *Scientific American* magazine, it was nicknamed the "Volcanic" because its rapid-fire sequence had the force of an erupting volcano! Other inventions of the

Smith & Wesson team included: the .22 rimfire revolver known as the Model 1; the Model 2, a larger-frame revolver that fired a .32 rimfire cartridge; and the large-caliber .44 revolver called the Model 3.

Naturally, as hired gunmen who were often employed by states, counties, and, in the case of rangers and marshals, the U.S. government, lawmen had their pick of the latest and greatest of these weapons. Gun manufacturers, in fact, courted the American military and indeed made much of their money off of lucrative government accounts. Many made their fortunes during the Civil War and the skirmishes with Native Americans that followed.

The Bowie knife was invented by Jim Bowie (inset), an American adventurer of the early 19th century who was killed at the Alamo in 1836. This long knife was a handy weapon for hand-to-hand fighting.

5 BEYOND BULLETS

DESPITE ALL THE GUNPLAY INVOLVED IN STORIES OF THE WILD WEST AND THE numerous advances made by gun manufacturers during this exciting time of exploration and discovery, not all weapons of the West needed gunpowder and bullets. After all, Native Americans had been living off the land and fighting amongst themselves for years before the white man introduced their "fire sticks," or guns. Living off the land and making the most of it, these resourceful Indians forged arrowheads out of flint rock and attached them to wooden shafts to make arrows. They also used other devices to fend off intruders, hunt, and find food. And while swords and bayonets proved to be limited during the Civil War, a man named James Bowie proved that knives could still be a formidable weapon once a man's bullets ran out!

Jim Bowie was a legendary figure of the western frontier who gave rise to such tall tales that it is now difficult for historians to separate fact from fiction. Scholars disagree on both the date and the place of his birth, but most agree that he was probably born in Kentucky in 1796. As a young boy, Jim and his family moved westward to find prosperity on the frontier. As he grew, Bowie became a prospector and a land speculator, living the rough life on the Texas border and finding himself in numerous fights.

Despite his roughneck existence and dangerous life, or perhaps because of it, Bowie is probably best remembered for his invention of a dangerous hunting knife, known as the Bowie knife. He is said to have introduced the long bolster, a protective, upturned piece of metal along the handle, to his knife to make it a better defensive weapon. Bowie is reported to have added this tool because he lost his grip on his old knife in a fight.

The invention of such a knife, which was also long, fierce, and intimidating looking, revived the lost art of knife fighting and made it an alternate form of self defense in a time of whizzing bullets and flying arrows. Knives were easy to conceal in boot legs or under jackets and could be just as deadly as bullets.

With the completion of the transcontinental railroad in 1867, the days of the Native Americans ranging freely through the West were already numbered. Native Americans often had to turn to violence when treaties with the U.S. Government were broken and their precious land was stolen. The American Indian tribes turned out to be formidable foes indeed. But the white man's guns were just one weapon in an arsenal overflowing with fierce objects that could harm and kill. In the West, the Plains Indians learned to fight from their horses.

The Native American coup stick was not really an effective weapon; it was used by Native Americans to show bravery in battle.

Each horseman attacked swiftly, often recklessly daring the fire of U.S. soldiers by seeking close combat in order to win honors by striking, or counting, coup.

Warriors of the plains made their coup sticks from wooden poles that were about six feet long and decorated with feathers or bits of animal skins. Striking an enemy with a coup stick or other weapon was the highest symbol of bravery, because it involved such close and dangerous contact. Some scholars believe that these coup sticks were a holdover

Geronimo and other well-armed Apaches appear to be ready for a fight in this 1886 photograph. The notorious Apache leader is holding an 1864 Springfield carbine.

It wasn't just men who could handle firearms. **Annie Oakley** gained the nickname "Little Sure Shot" for her skill with a rifle and shotgun. She was born Phoebe Ann Moses in Ohio in 1860. She learned to shoot by the time she was eight years old and helped support her family by hunting wild animals for a hotel in Cincinnati. In 1876, she adopted the stage name Annie Oakley and took part in shooting exhibitions. She and her husband, Frank Butler, soon joined Buffalo Bill Cody's famous Wild West Show. Part of Annie's act was to shoot a dime out of Frank's hand or a cigarette out of his mouth. Oakley could also hit a playing card thrown into the air 90 feet away! Like many characters from the old west, Annie earned a wild reputation. A popular musical comedy called *Annie Get Your Gun* portrays her as an outspoken tomboy. In reality, however, she was a quiet, simple person who even did needlepoint in her spare time.

from when the Indians fought hand-to-hand against each other with clubs and sharpened sticks.

Before Native Americans had access to firearms, their weapons were arrows, clubs, tomahawks, knives, and lances. Arrows could be as different from each other as the members

The Remington double-barreled derringer could be a dangerous weapon. Although it was not accurate at a range beyond a few yards, its small size meant that it could be easily concealed. This .41 caliber pistol was used to assassinate President William McKinley in September 1901.

of each individual tribe, but the arrowheads were usually either narrow and slim or triangular and thick. The triangular arrowheads were most often used in battle, where they would be loosely attached to the shaft of the arrow. This trick allowed many such arrowheads to remain in the wound, even after the wooden shaft was removed. Some Indians cut grooves down the shaft of their arrows to make it easier for blood to flow from the wound.

The bows were made of treated, sturdy wood and weathered, leather thongs strung tightly and worn in over months of constant use. By the time the western frontier opened up, guns—more importantly repeating rifles—became common. Naturally, bows and arrows became less effective against these powerful firearms. However, skilled Indians learned to conduct surprise attacks with their deadly bows and arrows.

The war club was another wicked weapon in the Native Americans' arsenal. At first, these clubs were simply a length of wood with a knob at the end. Over time, sharp bits of stone or bone were added to the tip. Later, as steel and other forms of metal became available, blades and spikes were used. Eventually, these war clubs developed into tomahawks, a hatchet-shaped weapon that was originally made of stone. After the Europeans came, the blades were often metal. Some were actually made in Europe.

For fighting from a distance, many warriors used weapons known as lances. These striking sticks were long poles, often up to 12 feet long, with large stone or metal points on the end. These points were shaped much like arrowheads and the poles themselves were often decorated with fur, eagle feathers and beads. Because of their length, fighting with lances was a difficult task attempted only by well-trained warriors.

Although the West was a dangerous place in the second half of the 19th century, by 1890 the frontier had disappeared. Once-lawless boom towns had become thriving communities filled with law-abiding citizens who would not tolerate reckless gunplay. The era of weapons of the West was over.

GLOSSARY

Border style
A type of draw in which the gunman reaches across his body to pull his gun, which is worn backward in its holster.

Cowboy
A person who works tending cattle or horses.

Crossdraw
A type of holster that allows the butt of the pistol to face forward.

Cylinder
The part of a revolver that holds the bullets and spins as each shot is taken.

Double-action
A type of revolver in which the pull of the trigger moves the cylinder into position and cocks the hammer.

Flintlock
A type of pistol in which a small piece of flint is used to ignite the gunpowder.

Gunpowder
The substance that ignites in a gun, causing a bullet to be fired.

Holster
The carrying case for a revolver or pistol.

Musket
A single-shot gun, popular during the Civil War era, that required the user to reload after every shot.

Outlaw
A person who lives outside of the law.

Pony Express
A mail delivery service in the West in the 1860s that featured men on horseback passing mail by relay across the country.

Posse
A group of people who work to help a lawman in an emergency.

Revolver
A gun with a revolving cylinder that holds bullets, allowing a person to fire several shots without reloading.

Rifle
A long-barreled gun that was more accurate than most revolvers.

Single-action
A type of revolver in which the cylinder is moved into position by the gunman cocking the hammer on the gun.

Six-shooter
A revolver that could hold six bullets.

TIMELINE

1816

Remington-made rifles get their start when young Eliphalet Remington II enters a shooting match with a new flintlock rifle he crafted in his father's forge located at Ilion Gulch, New York.

1836

Samuel Colt is issued a U.S. patent for the Colt firearm, equipped with a revolving cylinder containing five or six bullets.

1852

Horace Smith and Daniel B. Wesson, of Smith & Wesson fame, form their first partnership to manufacture a lever-action pistol.

1854

Winchester Firearms introduces its volcanic repeating handguns.

1860

The Henry rifle is patented by B. Tyler Henry.

1862

The first Henry rifles are sold.

1862

Congress passes the Homestead Act, which allows citizens to settle on up to 160 acres of unclaimed public land and receive title to it after living there for five years.

1865

The partnership of E. Remington & Sons was incorporated.

1866

Jesse and Frank James launch their legendary criminal career with a bank robbery at Liberty, Missouri.

1866

The Model 1866 "Yellow Boy" lever action rifle is introduced, the first gun to bear the Winchester name.

1867

The Colt company begins producing Doctor R. J. Gatling's machine gun, a semiautomatic weapon using a hand-operated crank to turn a cluster of six to 10 barrels while feeding ammunition into the breech.

1873

The Model 1873 lever action rifle is introduced by Winchester Firearms. No rifle came to symbolize the romance of the West more than this gun.

1876

The Model 1876 lever action rifle is introduced by Winchester Firearms.

1881

Legendary outlaw Billy the Kid is killed by Sheriff Pat Garrett.

1882

Jesse James, the notorious outlaw, is shot in the back by Robert Ford, a kinsman who hoped to collect a $5,000 reward.

1887

The Model 1887 lever action shotgun is introduced by Winchester Firearms.

1894

The Model 1894 lever action rifle is introduced by Winchester Firearms.

FURTHER READING

Athearn, Robert G. *American Heritage Illustrated History of the United States, Volume 6: The Frontier*. New York, NY: Silver Burdett Press, Inc., 1989.

Britten, Loretta and Mathless, Paul. *Our American Century: Prelude to the Century, 1870-1900*. Alexandria, VA: Time-Life Books, 1970.

Glackens, Ira. *Did Molly Pitcher Say That?* New York, NY: Writers & Readers Publishing, Inc., 1988.

Morison, Samuel Eliot. *The Oxford History of the American People, Volume Three: 1869 Through the Death of John F. Kennedy, 1963*. New York, NY: Penguin books USA Inc., 1994.

Newark, Peter. *Cowboys*. New York, NY: Bison Books Corporation, 1983.

Taylor, William O. *With Custer on the Little Bighorn: A Newly Discovered First-Person Account*. New York, NY: Penguin Books USA Inc., 1996.

Trachtman, Paul. *The Gunfighters: Showdowns and Shootouts in the Old West*. Alexandria, VA: Time-Life Books, 1974.

Ward, Geoffrey C. *The West: An Illustrated History*. New York, NY: The West Book Project, Inc., 1996.

INTERNET RESOURCES

Information about the Wild West

Samuel Colt

http://www.simonpure.com/colt.htm

http://www.netstate.com/states/peop/people/ct_sc.htm

http://www.colt.com/colt/html/i1a_historyofcolt.html

Weapons of the West

http://www.gunsoftheoldwest.com/

http://oseda.missouri.edu/~kate/guardians/maddock/info/info-guns.html

Gunfighters

http://history.cc.ukans.edu/heritage/research/gunfighters.html

http://www.linecamp.com/museums/americanwest/western_clubs

http://www.sptddog.com/sotp/gunfighters.html

http://www.nmsu.edu/~redtt/Resources/html/Outlaws.html

http://www.auschron.com/issues/vol15/issue2/arts.books.html

The gunfight at the O. K. Corral

http://www.tombstone.250x.com/index.html

http://www.AmericanWest.com/pages/docholid.htm

http://users.techline.com/nicks/earp.htm

http://www.clantongang.com/oldwest/gunfight.html

http://www.ukans.edu/heritage/gunfighters/okcorral.html

Information about the Wild West

http://www.discovery.com/guides/history/historybuff/library/refwest.html

http://www.finditquick.com/topics/5/59.html

http://www.thehistorynet.com/

INDEX

PHOTO CREDITS

2: Denver Public Library
6-7: Richard A. Cooke/Corbis
10: both North Wind Picture Archives
11: all Arizona Historical Society
14: (top) Hulton/Archive; (center) Arizona Historical Society; (bottom) Arizona Historical Society
16: Bettmann/Corbis
19: Arizona Historical Society
21: Richard A. Cooke/Corbis
26: Darrell Gulin/Corbis
28: James L. Amos/Corbis
31: Corbis
32: Denver Public Library
36-37: Hulton/Archive
40: Corbis
41: National Archives
44: North Wind Picture Archives
46: St. Joseph Museum, St. Joseph, Missouri
48: Michael Freeman/Corbis; (inset) Texas State Library and Archives Commission
51: Art Resource, NY
52: Arizona Historical Society
53: Denver Public Library
54: Hulton/Archive

Cover photos:
(front) Darrell Gulin/Corbis
(back) Denver Public Library

ABOUT THE AUTHOR

Rusty Fischer is the author of more than 100 published articles, essays, stories, and poems, which have appeared everywhere from national periodicals such as *Good Housekeeping* to best-selling anthologies such as *Chicken Soup for the Preteen Soul*. Most recently, he has authored four of the popular reference guides in the successful BUZZ ON series: *The Buzz on Dating, The Buzz on Fashion, The Buzz on Travel*, and *The Buzz on Fitness*. He is also the author of the best-selling series for students and teachers of reading and writing, *Creative Writing Made Easy*, published by Frank Schaffer Publications.